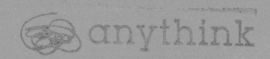

Earth Debates

How Harmful Are Fossil Fuels?

Catherine Chambers

heinemann
raintree

Edited by Helen Cox Cannons and Jill Kalz
Designed by Steve Mead
Original illustrations © Capstone Global Library Limited 2015
Illustrated by HL Studios, Witney, Oxon
Picture research by Tracy Cummins
Production by Helen McCreath
Originated by Capstone Global Library Limited
Printed and bound in China by CTPS

18 17 16 15 14
10 9 8 7 6 5 4 3 2 1

Library of Congress Cataloging-in-Publication Data
Chambers, Catherine, 1954-
  How harmful are fossil fuels? / Catherine Chambers.
    pages cm.—(Earth debates)
 ncludes bibliographical references and index.
ISBN 978-1-4846-0997-2 (hb)—ISBN 978-1-4846-1002-2 (pb)—ISBN 978-1-4846-1012-1 (ebook) 1. Fossil fuels—Environmental aspects—Juvenile literature. I. Title.
  TP318.3.C53 2015
  553.2—dc23   2014013812

This book has been officially leveled by using the F&P Text Level Gradient™ Leveling System.

Acknowledgments
We would like to thank the following for permission to reproduce photographs: AP Images: Press Association, 14; Capstone: HL Studios, 5, 6, 20; Corbis: © Adam Burton/Robert Harding World Imagery, 9, © AP Photo/ Charles Rex Arbogast, 31, © Imaginechina, 19, © Tom Fox/Dallas Morning News, 11; Getty Images: ANDEL NGAN/AFP, 10, Arnaldur Halldorsson/Bloomberg, 40, Asim Hafeez/ Bloomberg, 30, 36, Bartek Sadowski/Bloomberg, 21, Central Press/Hulton Archive, 24, Ed Reschke, 4, Norm Betts/Bloomberg, 15, 17, peisen zhao, 22, Ulrich Baumgarten, 39, Wade Payne/ Bloomberg, 27, William Thomas Cain, 23; Newscom: Dominique Leppin, 38, T Parisienne/Splash News, 13; Shutterstock: Art Konovalov, 33, bikeriderlondon, 29, fkdkondmi, Cover, Gary Whitton, 35, 37, John Carnemolla, 32, leonello calvetti, Cover, LEXXIZM, 25, Nightman1965, 12, Paul J Martin, 26, puchan, 28, Smileus, 7, straga, 8, Volodymyr Goinyk, 34; Thinkstock: Joe Gough, 16; U.S. Air Force: Joe Davila, 41.

We would like to thank Professor Daniel Block for his invaluable help in the preparation of this book.

Every effort has been made to contact copyright holders of material reproduced in this book. Any omissions will be rectified in subsequent printings if notice is given to the publisher.

All the Internet addresses (URLs) given in this book were valid at the time of going to press. However, due to the dynamic nature of the Internet, some addresses may have changed, or sites may have changed or ceased to exist since publication. While the author and publisher regret any inconvenience this may cause readers, no responsibility for any such changes can be accepted by either the author or the publisher.

Contents

Some words are shown in bold, **like this**. You can find out what they mean by looking in the glossary.

What Are Fossil Fuels?

The burning of fossil fuels—namely, coal, oil, and natural gas—provides almost 90 percent of the world's energy. At the moment, we consume more oil than coal or gas, but with new methods of extraction, natural gas is becoming more popular. Many scientists say that exploring, extracting, and burning fossil fuels all harm the planet. But is this the whole story? And where will our energy come from if we stop using fossil fuels?

To understand how our use of fossil fuels affects our planet, we must first look at how they formed and where they are found. So, let's go back about 325 million years, when Earth was a warm, swampy place covered in thick vegetation. Prehistoric creatures roamed the land and swam in the seas. Masses of tiny organisms floated on top of the oceans. Earth's landmasses heaved with earthquakes, volcanoes, and land shifts.

⌃ Ancient fossils of fern-like plants can be found in coal seams.

Did you know?

Fossil fuels are **nonrenewable**. But how much of a problem is this? With oil, for example, we are producing and using 32 billion barrels per year. As extraction becomes more difficult, costs rise. New technology should allow us to find fresh oil fields, but **renewable** forms of energy, such as Sun, wave, and wind power, might replace oil anyway.

Gradually, living creatures and plants died in the billions and were broken down and buried under deep layers of warm mud, sand, and rocks. Pressure and extreme heat from Earth's movements transformed some of the dead plant material into reserves of coal. Later, about 298 million years ago, it is thought that simple sea creatures and other living things changed into oil. Natural gas formed alongside coal and oil. Some of these fossil fuels were deposited close to Earth's surface. Others were laid down much deeper or beneath the ocean floor.

⋙ This is where we find coal today.

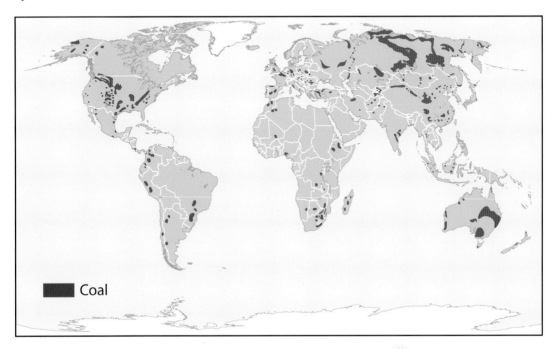

Coal

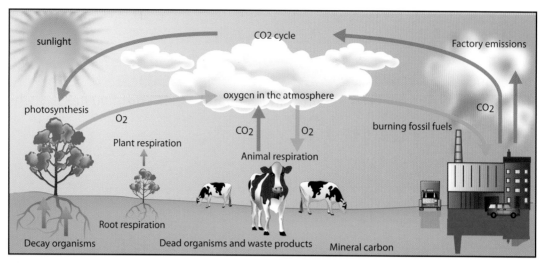

⌃ This **carbon cycle** diagram shows how carbon dioxide (CO_2) rises into the atmosphere. Plants back on Earth then absorb the CO_2. Plants use CO_2 and sunlight to make energy for growth.

So, how could fossil fuels be a problem?

Most fossil fuels lie deep under layers of rock, sand, and mud. Exploring and extracting them can be difficult. The methods and machinery used often harm animals and plants. In turn, this can affect humans who rely on a clean environment for their food or livelihood. Sometimes the visible landscape is scarred, too.

But many countries rely on fossil fuels to keep industry going and increase their wealth. Is this less important than preserving the natural environment and those who depend on it?

"If you take the Intergovernmental Panel on Climate Change (IPCC) predictions, then by 2040 every summer in Europe will be as hot as it was in 2003—between 110°F [43°C] and 120°F [49°C]. It is not the death of people that is the main problem, it is the fact that the plants can't grow—there will be almost no food grown in Europe."

James Lovelock (born 1919), environmental scientist

What about Earth's atmosphere? All the creatures and plants that were broken down into fossil fuels contained carbons. When coal and oil are burned, these carbons are released as **carbon dioxide** gas that rises into the atmosphere. Some gases are **emitted** when fossil fuels are extracted, such as **methane** gas from coal mining. Burning coal also emits polluting gases such as **sulfur dioxide**.

Many scientists believe that these gases are a major cause of climate change, especially a rise in global temperatures. Later in this book, we will explore the harmful effects of these gases, and why some scientists do not agree that they cause global warming. But first, how do we extract fossil fuels, and what harm might this do?

⌄ These industrial chimneys release gases that harm the atmosphere or pollute the air we breathe.

What's the Harm in Extracting Coal?

Hard, chunky coal was formed from fern-like plants millions of years ago. It was laid down in thick layers called seams. Some seams are near Earth's surface, while others are buried deep underground. Some lie at different angles, while others lie horizontally. These characteristics lead to different forms of extraction. Coal is a popular fossil-fuel energy source because it is often the cheapest to extract. So, how do we extract coal, and how much harm does this do to the planet?

Some seams lie fairly close to Earth's surface. Machinery removes the layers of rock above these seams to access the coal. This method is called surface or open-pit mining and is used widely in the United States, United Kingdom, Australia, China, and South Africa. The biggest problem is that it destroys the surrounding natural habitat and landscape. The tools and transportation used for excavating need fuel, which adds to carbon emissions. Explosives used to access the coal add to the mix of **pollutants**.

⌄⌄ Open-pit coal mining scars the landscape and creates coal dust that can affect people in nearby communities as well as coal miners.

But surface mining has fewer harmful effects on the health of mine workers than underground extraction. In many countries, open-pit sites use monitoring equipment to check that noise levels and dust from coal and rock do not exceed permitted levels.

HERO OR VILLAIN?

Open-pit mining does not necessarily scar the landscape permanently. In the United Kingdom, topsoil covering the coal seam is carefully removed and cataloged. Then it is stored in mounds that hide the scar of the mine as coal is being extracted. The mounds also act as a noise buffer. Once the coal has been fully extracted, the soil is spread over the site again.

It takes 5 to 10 years for an open-pit mine like this one to recover and return to nature.

What happens deep underground?

There are different methods of underground mining, depending on the depth of the seam. In deep-shaft mining, modern machinery can now reach coal seams that lie up to 1 mile (1.5 kilometers) beneath the surface. A massive cutter then digs out access tunnels from the shaft. In longwall mining, an automatic, rotating cutter, called a shearing drum, slices up panels of coal that can be as much as 383 yards (350 meters) long.

The harm done by deep mining might not seem as obvious as open-pit mining. But the rocks and soil dug out to make shafts and tunnels are deposited at the surface in massive **spoil** banks. Harmful toxins are brought up with them, polluting the **groundwater** as rainfall washes them into the soil. The ground above deep mines becomes less stable, too.

Did you know?

On August 5, 2010, the main ramp into the San Jose mine in Chile collapsed. Thirty-three miners were trapped over 2,300 feet (700 meters) below ground. No one could contact them for 17 days, and another cave-in blocked the rescue tunnel. The miners survived for 18 days before food and water reached them. They were trapped for 69 days and were finally rescued on October 14.

⌃ Mountaintop mining companies remove the upper slopes of mountains. The coal waste is often dumped into nearby valleys, harming the natural environment.

⌃ In deep mines in South Africa, the air is humid and extremely hot.
Air-conditioning systems help to improve these conditions.

Miners underground are exposed to dust and toxins from the coal and surrounding rock. Gas explosions are another danger. Methane gas rises naturally from the coal as it is mined. Methane is highly explosive and has caused many mine disasters. The worldwide coal-mining industry is trying to reduce the danger by making sure there are plenty of ventilation shafts in mines to allow the methane out, and air to flow in.

Methane gas that reaches the surface can be captured as an energy source. But most is flared, or burned, producing carbon dioxide—a **greenhouse gas**. But since unburned methane is 23 times more likely to increase global warming than carbon dioxide, this should reduce the harm to the atmosphere. It still means that coal extraction is harmful.

Is Oil Extraction Really Harmful?

Oil is greasy and viscous, which means it is sticky, runny, and oozes. These qualities mean that oil coats everything it comes into contact with. It is also volatile (it catches fire easily) and toxic. These hazards make oil one of the most dangerous fossil fuels to explore and extract. And since the world uses about 90 million barrels of it every day, the planet is exposed to a huge risk of harm. But are the benefits worth the risks? Oil production is still very profitable, and in many places oil costs less to produce than **biofuels** that are grown from plants (see pages 36–37).

Oil reserves often lie deep underneath remote landscapes with rich natural habitats. From sandy deserts and river creeks to icy oceans and warm seas, oil exploration and extraction can have a huge and lasting impact on people and their environments.

⌄ This oil rig has been towed into Gdansk port in Poland from the open sea. Oil can be spilled while the rig is towed.

⌃ Sea mammals such as this beached whale easily get lost if oil location guns interrupt their senses.

But the problems begin before a single drop of oil is extracted, because even oil exploration can cause harm. To find oil in our oceans, large ships tow huge guns that fire blasts of air into the water, creating sound waves. The sound waves hit the seafloor and bounce back to the ship. Equipment on board analyzes the length of the waves. The waves' lengths are mapped out over a large area, giving a picture of the seafloor's rock formations. From this, geologists can see if a particular section of the seafloor is likely to hold oil reserves.

However, this procedure can be highly damaging to marine life—and especially to marine mammals such as whales, seals, and dolphins. The sound waves disrupt their sense of hearing, which they need to communicate, find their prey, and avoid predators.

Did you know?

A single oil survey in the ocean lasts up to three weeks and can cover as much as 600 miles (966 kilometers). The guns used to locate oil can create a sound-wave level of up to 250 decibels. A human ear can be damaged at an 85-decibel level over just eight hours!

15/17 PIPER-A

Oil exploration on land begins with ground, air, and satellite surveys to map the geology of a target area. Computer models show the potential size of the oil fields. Experimental deep holes are also drilled, using heavy machinery that churns up the environment and pollutes it with waste spoil from the shaft. However, even greater harm is caused once the drilling begins for real.

What harm can drilling do?

Drilling at sea can cause oil spills and leakages that **contaminate** the ocean and its wildlife, including billions of microscopic plankton that provide food for many sea creatures. Drilling on land can lead to groundwater contamination, as well as wastage when water is used to dislodge blockages in the oil well. All around the sites, the environment is scarred with access roads, truck tracks, airstrips, and buildings.

Did you know?

In the 1980s, the Piper Alpha oil platform off Scotland's North-Sea coast produced over 300,000 barrels of crude oil per day. However, in 1988, a gas leak caused an explosion and a raging fire. It was the worst oil-platform disaster ever recorded. Only 61 out of the 226 workers survived, and it took nearly three weeks to control the flames.

⌃ Oil riggers often have to work two to three weeks before returning to shore, and they often work at night. They are tested for physical and mental fitness before they are allowed onto the rig.

What about the harm to workers in the oil industry? Offshore oil platforms, or rigs, can be dangerous places—especially in areas such as the North Sea, where there are often severe winter storms. Oil platforms can come adrift or catch fire. Some helicopters transporting workers to and from the shore have crashed, with tragic loss of life.

BIOGRAPHY

Paul Carter (born 1969)

Paul Carter loved every minute of working on oil platforms around the world—in the heat of Nigeria's creeks, in Borneo's tropical rain forest, and in the frozen Russian tundra. He loved the danger and became a popular writer about his experiences. But he is also a big supporter of cleaner fuels. In 2009, he rode all around Australia on a motorcycle, developed by the University of Adelaide, that was fueled by cooking oil.

BIOGRAPHY

Kenule "Ken" Beeson Saro Wiwa
(1941–1995)

The writer Ken Saro Wiwa protested against damage caused by oil exploration in his Ogoni homeland in Nigeria. In the Niger Delta, oil spills have polluted mangrove swamps, fishing habitats, and farmland. The United Nations suggests it will take $1 billion and 30 years to clean up the Niger Delta. Saro Wiwa used poetry and peaceful protest to get the world's attention.

This is an oil refinery in Australia. Oil has to be refined, or cleaned up, before it can be used. Oil refineries can produce a lot of toxic wastewater sludge.

How harmful is oil transportation?

We sometimes see the disastrous results of major oil leaks, spills, and fires on the television news. Most of these accidents happen while oil is being transported from wells to refineries and then to power plants or service stations in tankers, pipelines, and trucks.

One of the biggest spills occurred in 1989, when the tanker *Exxon Valdez* split open, spilling 11 million gallons (41.8 million liters) of oil, and damaging 1,300 miles (2,092 kilometers) of Alaskan coastline. However, some experts in oil exploration believe that oil theft from pipelines causes as much harm to the environment as oil spills. Nevertheless, between 1970 and 2013, about 40 million barrels of oil were spilled from tankers alone. Some of the biggest spills have happened during wars, such as the First Gulf War in Kuwait. The rest is natural seepage from oil sources.

Did you know?

Plans are in place to build the 1,179-mile (1,897-kilometer) Keystone XL oil pipeline from Canada's tar sands to the United States. The tar sands shown here are in Alberta, Canada. There's a danger that many oil leaks could occur in such a long pipeline. Oil from tar sands is extracted from thick, sticky bitumen mixed with sand. The extraction process pollutes nearby habitats and emits a lot of carbon dioxide. But extracting oil and tar from sand is increasingly popular as other oil reserves become harder to reach.

What's the Harm in Extracting Gas?

Can exploring, extracting, and transporting natural gas harm the planet? Many environmentalists would argue that it can. Yet the gas industry and some governments argue that gas is a "clean energy" because gas does not release much carbon dioxide when it is burned. Who is right? Natural gas is as cheap to extract as oil, so can we afford to stop exploiting it?

As with oil exploration, the size of a natural gas field is assessed using ground, air, and satellite imaging and computer modeling. There is also experimental drilling. Computer models are not always right, so drilling stops if the gas field turns out to be small. On land, this leaves a lot of holes, toxic spoil banks, and a damaged habitat.

Did you know?

Researchers from Boston University and North Carolina's Duke University have located almost 6,000 gas leaks in the underground pipeline system in Washington, D.C. Risks are high and include explosions and health hazards.

Established gas fields cause similar hazards to the environment—only on a much larger scale. Soil erosion is added to the mix. As gas is explored, toxins are drawn up with water, mud, and sludge and are contained in nearby evaporation ponds and pits. During the drilling itself, one of the most hazardous toxins is **radioactive** radon gas, which occurs naturally in rocks and soils around the gas pocket. Site workers inhaling the gas are at increased risk of lung cancer.

∧ A new pipeline stretches over 435 miles (700 kilometers) from Myanmar to China. Environmentalists fear for sensitive marine, mountain, and forest habitats.

Surely gas cannot pollute as much as oil?

Gas pollution is silent and invisible—but it is real! Gas is especially dangerous during transportation and processing. During processing, impurities from the natural gas are removed. These impurities include **hydrogen sulfide**, **helium**, carbon dioxide, other nonmethane **hydrocarbons**, and moisture, and they are harmful if they escape. Pipelines then transport the gas to power plants. Any fractures in the pipes can leak out dangerous methane emissions.

What's the fuss about fracking?

Many people from all parts of the world are protesting against fracking. So, what are their concerns? Fracking is hydraulic fracturing. In this process, water pressure is used to break up rock, releasing minute pockets of natural gas. The type of rock holding the gas is called Marcellus shale, a layer that lies at least 1 mile (1.6 kilometers) underground.

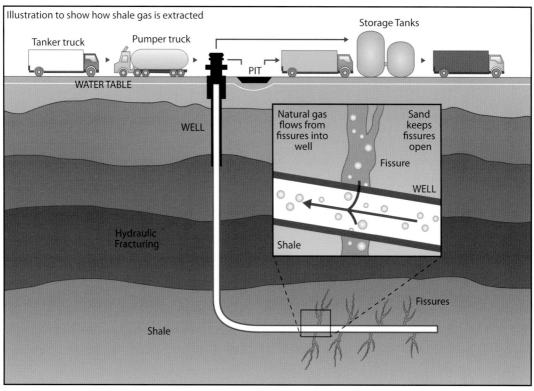

Illustration to show how shale gas is extracted

Storage Tanks

Tanker truck   Pumper truck

PIT

WATER TABLE

WELL

Natural gas flows from fissures into well

Sand keeps fissures open

Fissure

WELL

Hydraulic Fracturing

Shale

Shale

Fissures

⌃ Most of the fracking process is underground and unseen. This means it is hard to assess the environmental impact.

Did you know?

In Texas, media reports claimed that during November 2013, 16 earthquakes rocked the state. Many blamed fracking. But geologists at the U.S. Geological Survey believe that dumping the wastewater from fracking deep underground in empty wells could be the problem.

Each well is drilled vertically until the shale is reached. Then, it is drilled horizontally along the band of shale for a distance of about a quarter of a mile (400 meters). This broad band of rock is then shattered by up to 6 million gallons (23 million liters) of water plus sand and chemicals to expose the gas.

Those who oppose fracking argue that it can cause air and groundwater pollution, including radioactivity from wastewater. Fracking has also been blamed for earth tremors. Exploring and exploiting shale gas requires a lot of heavy machinery that disturbs nearby residents and wildlife. Shale workers on-site are exposed to toxins, such as silica dust, that can cause lung diseases.

⌄ This fracking site is in the province of Lublin, in Poland.

How Harmful Is Burning Coal Today?

Coal burns with a bright, hot flame that has brought warmth and light to people for hundreds of years. It fueled steam engines and the birth of the railroad. **Coke**, a form of burned coal, was used to smelt iron to build ships and machinery. But as the numbers of factories and trains increased, so did the volume of emissions. Coal's toxic soot emissions stuck to buildings—and inside human lungs. The development of coal-fired power stations added to the problem.

Coal creates the most harmful emissions of all the fuels used in power stations. Each coal-fired power station produces nearly twice as much carbon dioxide as it does natural gas, plus 12 times the amount of sulfur dioxide and five times the amount of **nitrogen oxide** for the amount of energy created. Some types of coal, called "high sulfur," have been cleaned so that they are less harmful. But they still emit damaging gases. What do these gases do?

⌄ This modern iron-smelting furnace injects a less harmful type of **pulverized coal**. Coal pollutes less than coke in the iron-smelting process.

22

⌃ This 19th-century stone house in Bath, England, has not yet been cleaned up after years of past coal burning, which polluted the air.

We know about the link between increased carbon-dioxide levels and climate change. However, sulfur dioxide affects us at ground level, increasing breathing problems such as asthma.

When nitrogen oxide combines with other **compounds**, it reacts with sunlight to create ground-level **ozone gas**. This causes severe breathing problems for some people. Nitrogen oxide harms the atmosphere, too. It is one of the gases that destroy the atmosphere's **ozone layer**, which protects Earth from the Sun's harmful rays. Levels of these gases have shrunk over the last 40 years in places where power plants have captured and recycled the gases.

Did you know?

How do power plants work? First, they need fuel to burn, such as coal. The heat from the burning coal boils water to create steam. The steam rises and presses against the blades of turbines, making them spin. The blades are connected to generators that create electricity.

Sulfur dioxide and nitrogen oxide become even more harmful when they react with water, oxygen, and other chemicals in the atmosphere and fall as "acid rain"—or acid hail or snow. When this toxic substance mixes with fog, it forms a thick, polluting, deadly smog.

London's Great Smog of 1952, in which an estimated 4,000 people died, led to the United Kingdom's Clean Air Acts of 1956, 1968, and 1993. UK law now insists that only low-smoke coals, such as anthracite, are burned in crowded city areas.

Eyewitness

During the Great London Smog, which began on December 4, 1952, there was no escaping the foul-smelling, sulfurous air. Stan Cribb, an undertaker, remembers, "You couldn't see a hand in front of you. Not only did you have this thick, black, curling smoke—it crept in everywhere, even the home—lace curtains thick with this oily substance."

But in many countries, there are no such laws, or the laws are poorly enforced. For example, coal emissions contribute to China's estimated 350,000 deaths each year from air pollution.

˅ Acid rain can fall on lakes and coastal bays, reducing oxygen in the water. Fish and marine plants need oxygen to survive. Water quickly becomes stagnant without it.

What happens to piles of ash waste?

Coal-fired power-plant sites contain piles of ash waste that can fill nearby ponds with toxic **metal oxides** and **alkalis**. In addition, the huge mounds of coal on these sites contain traces of arsenic and lead. Falling rain soaks through the coal piles and may trickle into river systems and lakes, carrying harmful toxins to fish and other wildlife. The toxins may also soak into the soil and pollute the groundwater. But even worse things can happen.

≫ China plans to build 160 new coal-fired power plants, adding to the 620 already operating. The country is searching for new technology to help reduce emissions.

Did you know?

In 2012, the International Energy Agency published a list of the world's top-ten coal producers. China heads the list.

Top-ten world coal producers, in tons			
PR China	3.8 billion	Russia	368 million
United States	1.1 billion	South Africa	279 million
India	645 million	Germany	208 million
Australia	456 million	Poland	158 million
Indonesia	414 million	Kazakhstan	129 million

∧ Ash sludge from the spill at the TVA Kingston coal plant polluted the land with toxic metals.

On December 22, 2008, an enormous ash spill occurred at the Tennessee Valley Authority (TVA) Kingston coal-fired power plant in Harriman, Tennessee. After 10 days of ceaseless rain, a wall holding back a spoil bank of toxic ash sludge collapsed. It flooded 12 homes, flowed into a nearby lake, and polluted the Emory River, killing hundreds of fish. It is estimated that over 1 billion gallons (3.8 billion liters) of ash sludge spilled over 300 acres (121 hectares).

HERO OR VILLAIN?

Coal and coal products have created a lot of wealth. Some of the emissions they produce are now recycled. For example, ash is used in cement and other building materials. Coking coal, important in steel production, has excellent heat-shielding properties, too. New energy-saving, coke-fueled steel furnaces have also been developed.

Does Burning Oil Harm the Planet?

Where would we be without oil? It gives us light and heat, as well as energy for industry. It fuels vehicles that allow us to travel quickly and in comfort. But what harm is our use of oil doing to the planet—and to us?

Does driving motor vehicles cause more harm than any other use of oil? Most scientists say it does. First, burning gasoline and **diesel oil** creates gas emissions from vehicles' exhaust systems. These gases include carbon dioxide, carbon monoxide, sulfur dioxide, nitrogen oxide, and water vapor. Second, vehicles emit particulates, which are minute pieces of solid matter.

⌄ Jet aircraft today emit fewer harmful gases per journey than they did 50 years ago. But there are a lot more journeys!

Did you know?

Crude oil is processed into several different fuels: gasoline and diesel fuel for road vehicles, jet fuel for aircraft, heating fuel, and **liquefied petroleum gas** (**LPG**), which can be used in vehicles or for heating. Each fuel emits different quantities of harmful gases.

We breathe in all these substances—and more! If we are exposed to a lot of them over a long period of time, they can increase our risk of heart disease, asthma, and lung cancer. People who are already sick are at more risk. So, too, are the very young and the very old.

Which fuel causes the most harm? Diesel was once thought to be a cleaner fuel than gasoline because it emits less carbon dioxide. But it has been discovered that diesel fumes contain harmful pollutants that gasoline does not—some of which are more likely to cause cancers. Diesel fumes can also create smog.

Oil-fired power plants are expensive to build and maintain.

Do oil-fired power plants harm the planet?

Oil-fired power plants generate large amounts of energy very quickly. They can be built anywhere that has good transportation links and a generous supply of water for cooling. But in addition to greenhouse gas emissions, oil-fired power stations create toxic sludge and wastewater from cooling. These waste products are hard to clean up, recycle, or throw away.

What happens when we burn oil waste?

Fierce debates surround the type of oil extracted from Canada's tar sands (see page 17). This thick, sticky bitumen oil needs to be thinned and separated in special refineries before it can be burned. This produces emissions and wastes that are hard to dispose of.

A particular problem is the hard, coal-like waste substance called "petcoke" (petroleum coke). When it burns, petcoke emits several times more carbon dioxide and sulfur dioxide than the oil from which it comes. The United States and Canada will not use petcoke, so it is exported to developing countries for them to burn instead. This adds to these countries' carbon footprints and health problems.

HERO OR VILLAIN?

Some climatologists say that **nuclear-fueled** power plants are cleaner than oil-fired plants and would be less harmful to the planet. But nuclear plants use **uranium**, which is nonrenewable and hazardous. Nuclear waste is radioactive, highly dangerous, and hard to dispose of safely. Which would you choose?

The United States needs to import nearly 9 billion barrels of oil a day and burns over 1 billion tons of coal every year. So, some leaders in industry and government are in no hurry to stop refining and using tar sands oil just because it produces petcoke. Do the needs outweigh the harm?

⌄ Canada has nearly 85 million tons of petcoke piles. In the United States, one oil refinery in Detroit, Michigan, processes 28,000 barrels of tar-sands oil per day, creating nearby spoil banks. In Chicago, Illinois, petcoke piles have caused alarming levels of toxic dust and runoff into rivers.

Is Natural Gas a "Clean" Form of Energy?

The natural gas industry claims that it is a very clean form of energy. When burned, it produces less of the greenhouse gas carbon dioxide than other fossil fuels. It has low nitrogen oxide and produces virtually no sulfur dioxide emissions or mercury, so it won't contribute to poor air quality, smog, or polluted waterways. But is this the whole story?

Natural gas is made up mostly of methane. This has a Global Warming Potential (GWP) 20 times that of carbon dioxide over a 100-year period. But this is only if it escapes as it is being explored, transported, or stored, or if there are leaks at gas power plants. Even then, methane is thought to last in the atmosphere for only 20 years, which is many times less than carbon dioxide.

⌄ Methane gases from livestock make up about 10 percent of Australia's greenhouse gases. Cattle from northern Australia produce half of this amount!

Natural gas is not the only fuel that leaks methane. Petroleum oil and coal do, too. Together, they produce over 40 percent of all methane emissions in the United States. But the rest comes from natural sources such as decaying bacteria in wetlands, decaying matter in landfill sites, and a lot from stomach gases of livestock such as cattle!

But what harm does natural gas do when it is burned? Natural gas power stations still emit carbon dioxide through their chimneys. The burning process produces a lot of polluted wastewater that gets discharged into rivers and lakes. In the home, gas heating and cooking systems emit toxins that are harmful to the lungs, including tiny solid particles, carbon monoxide, and nitrogen oxide.

⩔ There is a lot of pressure to change truck fuel from diesel to natural gas. But many scientists argue that unless methane leaks are plugged, natural gas will be a worse pollutant than diesel.

What Can We Use Instead of Fossil Fuels?

What will we do when fossil fuels run out? Will this be a blessing to the planet? Or will it just mean that we are poorer? Some energy companies have developed alternatives. Others, however, are trying new ways to find fossil fuels in the toughest parts of the planet. Which way will it go? And which will do the least harm?

> **"Those who argue that we should stop exploring, harvest existing fields, and block new opportunities are, at best, preparing for a future that doesn't exist."**
>
> Helge Lund, chief executive officer of the energy company Statoil, speaking in 2013

⌄ In Antarctica, melting ice would make oil and gas exploration much easier. Will it ever happen?

Oil companies such as France's Total say they are too worried about spills to drill here in Arctic Alaska.

When will fossil fuels run out? Many who are in favor of fossil fuels believe that they will last for a very long time because new sources are constantly being found. Those who prefer carbon-free energy say they will all be gone by 2088! But, for now, fossil fuel exploration is taking place in some of the most sensitive natural environments, including the Arctic. Here, many local communities worry about the **ecological** effects of leaks and spills.

Is the clean, wild Antarctic region safe? So far, the area is protected from mining by an agreement called the Madrid Protocol that was signed in 1998 by all countries with an interest in the region. However, the ban on mining in the Antarctic will be reviewed in 2048. Do you think the need for fuels will win out over protecting the environment?

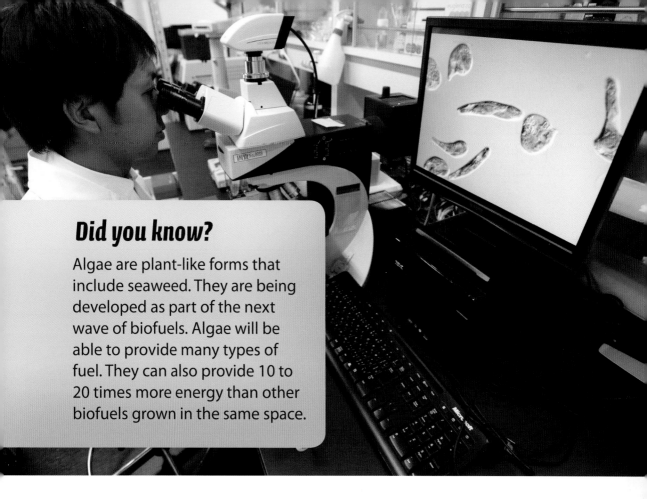

What's the harm in growing fuels?

Are plants the answer? Wood has provided fuel since humans discovered how to make fire. Wood is still a useful fuel as long as trees can be grown like a crop and replaced. However, as a fuel, wood emits a lot of carbon dioxide.

Today, other crops are grown for fuel called biofuels. They can be used to power both industry and vehicles. Some plants, such as sugarcane and wheat, produce sugar and starch that is fermented to make **ethanol**. Other crops, such as soybeans, corn, and palm, produce oils that are made into **biodiesel**. Biofuels can also be made from decaying waste plant and animal material. All these fuels together are known as **biomass**.

There are a lot of advantages to growing biofuels. Many scientists believe they are "carbon neutral" and will not contribute to climate change. Biofuels are also renewable.

However, there are also problems. Growing crops for biofuels takes up land that could be used for growing food. Large biofuel agricultural companies have pushed out smaller farmers. Big areas of rain forest have been cleared to make way for biofuel crops. Rain forests can absorb extra carbon dioxide from the atmosphere, and cutting them back could affect the world's climates.

Plowing, sowing, and applying chemical fertilizers, pesticides, and herbicides all add to pollution and the carbon footprint of biofuels. They also use up a great deal of water. However, scientists are looking at ways to make fuels from the stalks of harvested crops, so no extra water or land would be needed.

⌄⌄ In Brazil, sugarcane is grown to make ethanol.

What about wind, waves, water, and the Sun?

For hundreds of years, people used the power of wind and water to drive the windmills and water mills that ground grain into flour. Today, we generate **hydroelectric power** (**HEP**) from fast-flowing river water as it passes through huge dams. Wind turbines and wave barriers along coastlines add to the power supply. The Sun's energy can be converted to electricity through **photovoltaic cells**. Wind, waves, water, and sunshine are all renewable sources of energy. So, what could be the problem?

Let us start with dams. When a dam is built to block the flow of a river, a huge lake of water builds up behind it. Electricity is generated when water from the lake is released through the dam and plunges downward, turning electric turbines below. But these huge, human-made lakes have flooded river valleys, destroyed wildlife and freshwater habitats, and forced people to leave their homes. Dams can also cut off water supplies farther down the river. For example, there are worries that Turkey's plans to dam the Euphrates and Tigris rivers will reduce water supplies to Syria and Iraq, which lie downstream.

≪ When really strong winds hit wind turbines, there is a danger they can catch fire.

⋀ Solar energy can power refrigerators and stoves in remote areas. Clinics can store vaccines in refrigerators to keep them fresh.

We can now harness the power of waves by anchoring turbines offshore in rows stretching across coastal bays. But protestors say that the turbines disrupt the habitat of sea creatures and harm the fishing industry.

Solar panels still cannot harness the Sun's energy at all times. It takes a lot of panels, and therefore a lot of land, to generate a strong, steady supply of electricity. Wind farms are also unable to supply more than a small percentage of our energy needs—and protestors complain that they ruin the landscape.

So, How Harmful Are Fossil Fuels?

We know that most scientists believe that burning fossil fuels causes or contributes to climate change. We know that when we exploit fossil fuels, humans and habitats are harmed. But we also know that alternative forms of energy cannot yet replace them. Fossil fuels are easier to use than nuclear fuel, and can produce more energy for the same amount of effort as renewable fuels. What is the best way forward?

⌄ There is a lot of volcanic activity in Iceland, which is used to produce **geothermal energy**.

> **Horses create 772 grams of pollution per kilometer traveled [for each horse galloping], modern cars only 72.4 grams per kilometer. The wellsite footprint for [oil] wells drilled at Prudhoe Bay [Alaska] has been reduced from 60 acres to 6 acres since 1970.**

Lee Gerhard (born 1937), retired geologist and climate change **skeptic**, 2001

Could rocket science help find fuels for Earth? A new rocket fuel called ALICE is being developed using aluminum powder and water ice.

BIOGRAPHY

James Hansen (born 1941)
James Hansen was director of NASA's Goddard Institute for Space Studies. He first warned the U.S. government of the dangers of climate change in 1988. However, he does not believe that renewable energy is the whole answer and supports more nuclear power plants.

We can all try to reduce our use of fossil fuels. We could travel by train, bus, or bicycle more often, and so reduce the number of cars on the roads. We could insulate our homes better so that we use less heating—or wear extra layers! We could remember to turn off lights and other electrical equipment when they are not in use. And we could reuse and recycle more household items to help cut down on fuels used to produce new goods. These are just a few of the things we could do to help.

But what about poorer countries that are trying to increase their wealth by developing their industries? Industry needs power, and these countries cannot afford to wait for cheap and effective alternatives to fossil fuels. There are no easy answers to the harm or problems created by fossil fuels.

Quiz

How much do you remember about fossil fuels from reading this book? You could find out by answering these questions. You can use the index to help you. Some of the answers might lie in the boxes and captions as well as the main text.

1   Which of these gases is not a fossil fuel?
   A coal
   B natural gas
   C ethanol
   D petroleum oil

2   What harm do too many greenhouse gases in Earth's atmosphere do?
   A They poison the air that we breathe.
   B They help plants to grow in greenhouses.
   C They are thought to contribute to climate change.
   D They stop the Sun's rays from reaching Earth.

3   Which type of petroleum oil is thick, sticky, and mixed with sand before it is processed?
   A oil found deep under the ocean
   B biofuel oil
   C oil that gets mixed with sand as it is transported
   D tar sands oil

4   What type of machine is used to extract coal in the underground longwall mining method?
   A a pickaxe
   B a pneumatic drill
   C a rotating shearing drum
   D a triangular coal plow

5   The long 1,678-mile (2,700-kilometer) Keystone XL oil pipeline is being built between which two countries?
   A Australia and New Zealand
   B Canada and the United States
   C Russia and Canada
   D The United Kingdom and Poland

6 How far underground is Marcellus shale, a type of rock mined when fracking?

A 1 mile (1.6 kilometers)

B 1.5 miles (2.4 kilometers)

C 2 miles (3.2 kilometers)

D 4 miles (6.4 kilometers)

7 Energy plants powered by nuclear fuel are considered cleaner than those powered by fossil fuels. But which of these problems does nuclear fuel create?

A Nuclear fuel emits methane gas.

B Nuclear fuel creates dangerous radioactive waste.

C Nuclear fuel emits gases that cause lung disease.

D Nuclear fuel creates sooty particulates.

8 Particulates are emitted by burning fossil fuels. What are they, and what harm do they do?

A They are ozone gases that rise into the stratosphere, destroying the ozone layer.

B They are pieces of coal that can burn plants.

C They are greenhouse gases that can cause climate change.

D They are tiny solids, mainly carbons, that are released into the air, causing lung disease.

9 Which gas causes breathing problems and acid rain when coal is burned?

A Carbon dioxide is the cause.

B Sulfur dioxide is the cause.

C Oxygen is the cause.

D Helium is the cause.

10 Coal, oil, and natural gas produce 40 percent of all harmful methane gases released on Earth. What else releases methane gas?

A the stomachs of plant-eating livestock such as cattle

B rain forest trees

C photovoltaic cells used to create solar energy

D wind farms

ANSWERS: 1C, 2C, 3D, 4C, 5B, 6A, 7B, 8D, 9B, 10A

Glossary

alkali chemical in burned coal waste that can be toxic in water sources and in soil

biodiesel biofuel that can be used in diesel engines

biofuel renewable fuel made from plant matter

biomass fuel created using plant and animal matter

carbon cycle movement of carbon gases in a circle, emitted from carbon gases and absorbed by plant life and carbon sinks such as the oceans

carbon dioxide greenhouse gas released by burning fossil fuels; also one of several impure gases removed from natural gas fuel before it is used

coke type of coal made by burning coals, such as bituminous coal

compound substance made up of two or more chemical elements

contaminate when a toxic substance mixes with water, air, or soil, making it stale or poisonous

diesel oil fuel that is usually extracted from petroleum oil and used in diesel engines; it can also be extracted from plants (biodiesel)

ecological relation of living organisms to each other and their habitats

emit produce and give out something, usually a gas

ethanol biofuel made by fermenting starch from a plant, such as wheat

geothermal energy energy from volcanic sources

greenhouse gas gas that causes climate change, particularly global warming

groundwater underground water source

helium type of impure gas removed from natural gas fuel before it is used

hydrocarbon type of impure gas removed from natural gas fuel before it is used

hydroelectric power (HEP) power source that uses the force of water to turn turbines and create electric power

hydrogen sulfide type of impure gas removed from natural gas fuel before it is used

liquefied petroleum gas (LPG) type of gas from refined petroleum oil or certain forms of natural gas

metal oxide chemical in burned coal waste that can be toxic in water sources and in soil

methane greenhouse gas released by burning fossil fuels

nitrogen oxide polluting gas found in car exhausts

nonrenewable fuel type that can no longer be formed naturally or created artificially

nuclear fuel radioactive energy created by using uranium and plutonium chemical elements

ozone gas gas that can rise into the atmosphere and destroy the ozone layer

ozone layer layer of gases in the stratosphere that protects Earth from the Sun's harmful rays

photovoltaic cell manufactured cell in which the Sun's energy can be stored and used as a power source

pollutant toxic substance that can be harmful to the natural world, humans, and the atmosphere

pulverized coal powdered coal or coal dust

radioactive substance used in nuclear fuels that can create harmful rays if it is leaked

renewable fuel type that is formed naturally—for example, wind energy

skeptic someone who questions or doubts accepted opinions about a subject

solar panel panel of photovoltaic cells in which energy from the Sun can be stored and used

spoil waste from extracting or burning fossil fuels

sulfur dioxide polluting gas released by burning coal

uranium radioactive chemical element used in creating nuclear fuels

wellsite footprint amount of carbon emissions and damage around a well site

Find Out More

If you want to find out more about fossil fuels, take a look at some of these books, web sites, and places to visit.

Books

Gillett, Jack, and Meg Gillett. *Energy-Resource Maps* (Maps of the Environmental World). New York City: PowerKids, 2013.

Gogerly, Liz. *Fossil Fuels* (A World After). Chicago: Heinemann Library, 2014.

Hartman, Eve, and Wendy Meshbesher. *Climate Change* (Sci-Hi). Chicago: Raintree, 2010.

Spilsbury, Richard, and Louise Spilsbury. *Fossil Fuel Power* (Let's Discuss Energy Resources). New York City: PowerKids, 2012.

Web Sites

FactHound offers a safe, fun way to find Internet sites related to this book. All of the sites on FactHound have been researched by our staff.

Here's all you do:

Visit www.facthound.com

Type in this code: 9781484609972

Places to Visit

Local and national science and technology museums often feature exhibitions on the atmosphere, the environment, and climate change. For example, you can check out the following:

The Exploratorium, San Francisco, California
www.exploratorium.edu
The Exploratorium is a science museum with hands-on exhibits that encourage visitors to directly engage with science. Among its many fascinating exhibits about the environment is the Bay Observatory Gallery, which explores the surrounding San Francisco Bay area, including its ecology.

Museum of Science, Boston, Massachusetts
www.mos.org
The Museum of Science, Boston, features many exhibits that explore issues relating to the environment and problems affecting Earth. Check out "Catching the Wind," which explores the use of turbines and wind energy. "Conserve @ Home" shows you how you might be wasting energy in your home. "Energized!" explores natural energy sources such as the Sun, water, and wind.

The Museum of Science and Industry, Chicago, Illinois
www.msichicago.org
Here, you can explore the "Future Energy Chicago" exhibition. This begins with an explanation of different forms of energy and then allows visitors to compete to find the most environmentally friendly solutions to problems such as transportation, car design, and home design. "Earth Revealed" investigates different issues affecting our planet. The museum also features many revolving exhibits about climate and the environment.

Index